I0445158

DATA SCIENCE MASTERY

From Fundamentals to Advanced Techniques

Yatendra Kumar Singh 'Manuh'

Copyright © 2024 Yatendra Kumar Singh 'Manuh'

All rights reserved

The characters and events portrayed in this book are fictitious. Any similarity to real persons, living or dead, is coincidental and not intended by the author.

No part of this book may be reproduced, or stored in a retrieval system, or transmitted in any form or by any means, electronic, mechanical, photocopying, recording, or otherwise, without express written permission of the publisher.

Contact: manujadon007@hotmail.com

CONTENTS

Title Page
Copyright
Introduction
Chapter 1: Introduction to Data Science — 1
Conclusion — 4
Chapter 2: Data Science Toolkit — 5
Conclusion — 9
Chapter 3: Data Collection and Preprocessing — 10
Conclusion — 14
Chapter 4: Exploratory Data Analysis (EDA) — 15
Conclusion — 19
Chapter 5: Statistical Analysis for Data Science — 20
Conclusion — 25
Chapter 6: Introduction to Machine Learning — 26
Conclusion — 30
Chapter 7: Supervised Learning Algorithms — 31
Conclusion — 35
Chapter 8: Unsupervised Learning Algorithms — 36
Conclusion — 40
Chapter 9: Advanced Machine Learning Techniques — 41
Conclusion — 46

Chapter 10: Model Evaluation and Optimization	47
Conclusion	52
Chapter 11: Big Data and Data Engineering	53
Conclusion	58
Chapter 12: Time Series Analysis and Forecasting	59
Conclusion	63
Chapter 13: Data Science in Practice	64
Conclusion	69
Chapter 14: Data Visualization and Storytelling	70
Conclusion	75
Chapter 15: Introduction to Artificial Intelligence	76
Conclusion	80
Chapter 16: Deep Learning and Neural Networks	81
Conclusion	86
Chapter 17: Natural Language Processing (NLP)	87
Conclusion	91
Chapter 18: Reinforcement Learning	92
Conclusion	97
Chapter 19: Ethics and Bias in Data Science	98
Conclusion	103
Chapter 20: Capstone Project	104
Conclusion	109
Chapter 21: Future Trends in Data Science	110
Conclusion	114
Afterword	115

INTRODUCTION

In today's data-driven world, the ability to harness and analyze vast amounts of information has become a critical skill across various industries. Data science, a multidisciplinary field that combines statistical analysis, machine learning, and domain expertise, empowers organizations to make informed decisions, uncover hidden patterns, and drive innovation. "Data Science Mastery: From Fundamentals to Advanced Techniques" is your comprehensive guide to navigating the complexities of data science and unlocking its transformative potential.

This book is designed to take you on a journey from the foundational principles of data science to the cutting-edge techniques that are shaping the future of the field. Whether you are a novice looking to embark on a career in data science, a seasoned professional seeking to deepen your expertise, or a business leader aiming to leverage data for strategic advantage, this book offers valuable insights and practical knowledge.

Throughout the chapters, you will explore:

- **Foundational Concepts:** Gain a solid understanding of the core principles of data science, including data collection, preprocessing, and exploratory data analysis. Learn about the essential tools and programming languages that form the backbone of data science projects.

- **Advanced Techniques:** Delve into sophisticated machine learning algorithms, deep learning, natural language processing, and reinforcement learning. Discover how these advanced techniques can be applied to solve complex real-world problems.

- **Practical Applications:** Apply your knowledge through case studies and hands-on projects that demonstrate the practical applications of data science across different industries. Explore ethical considerations and best practices for responsible data science.

- **Future Trends:** Stay ahead of the curve by exploring emerging trends and technologies that are shaping the future of data science. Understand the impact of artificial intelligence, big data, and automation on the field.

Each chapter is crafted to provide you with a comprehensive understanding of the topic, supported by real-world examples, detailed explanations, and step-by-step guides. By the end of this book, you will have the skills and confidence to tackle data science challenges, drive data-driven decision-making, and contribute to the advancement of the field.

Join us on this exciting journey to master data science. Let's unlock the power of data and transform the way we understand and interact with the world.

CHAPTER 1: INTRODUCTION TO DATA SCIENCE

Overview of Data Science

Data science is an interdisciplinary field that combines statistical analysis, machine learning, and domain expertise to extract meaningful insights from data. By analyzing large volumes of data, data scientists can uncover patterns, identify trends, and make data-driven decisions that drive innovation and business growth. The field of data science encompasses various techniques and tools to process, analyze, and visualize data, making it a powerful tool for addressing complex problems across different industries.

Importance and Applications

The importance of data science cannot be overstated in today's digital age. Organizations across all sectors leverage data science to improve their operations, enhance customer experiences, and gain a competitive edge. Key applications of data science include:

- **Healthcare:** Predicting disease outbreaks, personalizing treatment plans, and improving patient care through predictive analytics and machine learning models.
- **Finance:** Detecting fraudulent transactions, managing risk, and optimizing investment strategies using advanced data analysis techniques.

- **Retail:** Enhancing customer experiences through personalized recommendations, optimizing inventory management, and analyzing consumer behavior.
- **Marketing:** Identifying target audiences, optimizing marketing campaigns, and measuring campaign effectiveness with data-driven insights.
- **Transportation:** Improving route planning, reducing fuel consumption, and enhancing safety through data analysis and predictive modeling.
- **Manufacturing:** Optimizing production processes, predicting maintenance needs, and improving product quality using data science techniques.

Skills Required for Data Science

A successful data scientist needs a diverse set of skills that span multiple disciplines. Key skills required for data science include:

- **Programming:** Proficiency in programming languages such as Python and R for data analysis, manipulation, and visualization.
- **Statistics and Mathematics:** A strong foundation in statistics and mathematics to perform data analysis, build models, and interpret results.
- **Machine Learning:** Understanding machine learning algorithms and techniques to create predictive models and automate decision-making processes.
- **Data Wrangling:** Ability to clean, preprocess, and transform raw data into a usable format for analysis.
- **Data Visualization:** Skills in creating visual representations of data to communicate insights effectively using tools like Matplotlib, Seaborn, and Tableau.
- **Domain Knowledge:** Understanding the specific industry or domain in which data science is applied to contextualize findings and make informed decisions.

Career Opportunities in Data Science

The demand for data scientists is growing rapidly as organizations recognize the value of data-driven decision-making. Career opportunities in data science are diverse and span various roles, including:

- **Data Analyst:** Focuses on analyzing data to identify trends, patterns, and insights that inform business decisions.
- **Data Engineer:** Builds and maintains data pipelines and infrastructure to support data analysis and machine learning workflows.
- **Machine Learning Engineer:** Designs and implements machine learning models and algorithms for predictive analytics and automation.
- **Business Intelligence Analyst:** Uses data to generate insights and support strategic business decisions through reporting and visualization.
- **Research Scientist:** Conducts advanced research in data science, machine learning, and artificial intelligence to develop new methodologies and technologies.
- **Data Science Consultant:** Provides expertise and guidance to organizations on how to leverage data science for business growth and innovation.

CONCLUSION

Chapter 1 provides an introduction to the field of data science, highlighting its importance, applications, required skills, and career opportunities. As you progress through this book, you will delve deeper into the various aspects of data science, gaining the knowledge and skills needed to excel in this dynamic and impactful field.

CHAPTER 2: DATA SCIENCE TOOLKIT

Programming Languages: Python and R

One of the foundational elements of data science is proficiency in programming languages. Python and R are the most widely used languages in the data science community, each offering unique strengths:

- **Python:**
    - **Versatility and Ease of Use:** Python's simple and readable syntax makes it an excellent choice for beginners and professionals alike. It's versatile, supporting various tasks from web development to data analysis.
    - **Extensive Libraries:** Python boasts a vast ecosystem of libraries and frameworks specifically designed for data science, such as NumPy, pandas, Matplotlib, Scikit-learn, TensorFlow, and PyTorch.
    - **Community Support:** Python has a large and active community, providing a wealth of resources, tutorials, and forums for troubleshooting and learning.
- **R:**
    - **Statistical Analysis:** R was designed for statistical computing and graphics, making

it a powerful tool for data analysis and visualization.
- **Comprehensive Packages:** R has an extensive collection of packages, such as ggplot2, dplyr, tidyr, and caret, which are tailored for various data science tasks.
- **Strong Community:** R's community is vibrant and continually contributes to the development of new packages and resources.

Data Science Libraries and Frameworks

Data science relies heavily on libraries and frameworks that simplify and enhance the process of data manipulation, analysis, and visualization. Key libraries and frameworks include:

- **NumPy:** A fundamental library for numerical computing in Python, providing support for arrays, matrices, and a wide range of mathematical functions.
- **pandas:** A powerful library for data manipulation and analysis, offering data structures like DataFrame, which allows for efficient handling of large datasets.
- **Matplotlib and Seaborn:** Libraries for creating static, interactive, and animated visualizations in Python. Matplotlib is highly customizable, while Seaborn builds on Matplotlib with a focus on statistical plotting.
- **Scikit-learn:** A comprehensive machine learning library in Python that provides simple and efficient tools for data mining, data analysis, and machine learning.
- **TensorFlow and PyTorch:** Leading deep learning frameworks that offer robust tools for building and training neural networks. TensorFlow, developed by Google, and PyTorch, developed by Facebook, are widely used in both research and industry.
- **ggplot2:** A data visualization package in R based on the Grammar of Graphics, allowing users to create complex and multi-layered visualizations with ease.

- **dplyr and tidyr:** Essential packages in R for data manipulation and cleaning, providing intuitive functions for filtering, selecting, and transforming data.

Tools for Data Analysis and Visualization

Data analysis and visualization tools play a crucial role in extracting insights and presenting data in a comprehensible manner. Key tools include:

- **Jupyter Notebooks:**
  - **Interactive Environment:** Jupyter Notebooks provide an interactive environment for running and sharing code, combining code execution, rich text, and visualizations in a single document.
  - **Support for Multiple Languages:** While primarily used with Python, Jupyter Notebooks also support R and other programming languages through kernels.
- **RStudio:**
  - **Integrated Development Environment (IDE):** RStudio is a powerful IDE for R, offering a user-friendly interface, code editor, and integrated tools for data analysis and visualization.
  - **Enhanced Productivity:** RStudio includes features like version control, project management, and package development support, enhancing productivity for data scientists.
- **Tableau:**
  - **Data Visualization Software:** Tableau is a leading data visualization tool that enables users to create interactive and shareable dashboards. It connects to various data sources and provides drag-and-drop functionality for

building visualizations.
- **Ease of Use:** Tableau's intuitive interface allows users to quickly create visualizations without extensive programming knowledge.

- **Apache Spark:**
  - **Big Data Processing Framework:** Apache Spark is a powerful engine for large-scale data processing, providing in-memory computing capabilities. It supports various data processing tasks, including batch processing, real-time streaming, and machine learning.
  - **Integration with Data Science Tools:** Spark integrates with data science languages like Python (using PySpark) and R (using SparkR), making it accessible to data scientists for big data analysis.

CONCLUSION

Chapter 2 introduces the essential tools and programming languages that form the backbone of data science. By mastering Python and R, leveraging key libraries and frameworks, and utilizing powerful tools for data analysis and visualization, you will be well-equipped to tackle data science challenges and derive meaningful insights from your data.

CHAPTER 3: DATA COLLECTION AND PREPROCESSING

Types of Data and Sources

Data collection is a critical step in the data science process, as the quality and accuracy of the collected data directly impact the insights and outcomes derived from it. Data can be categorized into different types based on its characteristics:

- **Structured Data:** Data that is organized into predefined formats, such as tables, with rows and columns. Examples include relational databases, spreadsheets, and CSV files.
- **Unstructured Data:** Data that does not have a predefined structure, such as text, images, audio, and video. Examples include social media posts, emails, and multimedia files.
- **Semi-Structured Data:** Data that does not fit neatly into structured formats but contains tags or markers to separate elements. Examples include JSON and XML files.

Data can be collected from various sources, including:

- **Internal Databases:** Data stored within an organization's databases, such as customer records, sales transactions, and inventory data.
- **Public Data Sources:** Data available from public

repositories and government databases, such as census data, economic indicators, and open data portals.
- **Web Scraping:** Extracting data from websites using automated scripts or tools, such as Beautiful Soup and Scrapy in Python.
- **APIs:** Accessing data through Application Programming Interfaces (APIs) provided by various services and platforms, such as social media APIs, financial data APIs, and weather APIs.
- **Sensors and IoT Devices:** Data collected from sensors and Internet of Things (IoT) devices, such as environmental sensors, wearable devices, and smart home gadgets.

Data Collection Methods

The methods used for data collection depend on the nature of the data and the sources from which it is being collected. Common data collection methods include:

- **Surveys and Questionnaires:** Collecting data directly from individuals through structured surveys and questionnaires. This method is useful for gathering qualitative and quantitative data.
- **Interviews and Focus Groups:** Conducting one-on-one interviews or group discussions to gather in-depth information and insights from participants.
- **Observational Studies:** Collecting data by observing and recording behaviors, events, or conditions without direct interaction with subjects.
- **Web Scraping:** Using automated scripts to extract data from websites, enabling the collection of large volumes of data quickly.
- **APIs:** Utilizing APIs to retrieve data from external services and platforms, allowing for real-time data collection and integration.

Data Cleaning and Preparation

Once data is collected, it needs to be cleaned and prepared for analysis. Data cleaning and preparation involve several steps to ensure the data is accurate, consistent, and ready for analysis:

1. **Handling Missing Data:**
    - **Identifying Missing Data:** Detect missing values in the dataset using techniques such as summary statistics and visualizations.
    - **Imputation:** Replace missing values with appropriate estimates, such as mean, median, mode, or using advanced techniques like K-Nearest Neighbors (KNN) imputation.
    - **Removing Missing Data:** Remove rows or columns with a high percentage of missing values, if they are not critical to the analysis.
2. **Dealing with Outliers:**
    - **Identifying Outliers:** Detect outliers using statistical methods, such as Z-scores and the IQR method, or visualizations like box plots.
    - **Handling Outliers:** Address outliers by removing them, transforming them, or using robust statistical methods that are less sensitive to outliers.
3. **Data Transformation:**
    - **Normalization and Standardization:** Scale numerical data to ensure that features have similar ranges, using techniques like Min-Max normalization and Z-score standardization.
    - **Encoding Categorical Data:** Convert categorical data into numerical format using techniques like one-hot encoding, label encoding, and binary encoding.
4. **Data Integration:**

- **Combining Datasets:** Merge multiple datasets from different sources to create a unified dataset for analysis. Ensure consistency and resolve any conflicts or discrepancies between datasets.
- **Data Aggregation:** Aggregate data at different levels of granularity to create summary statistics or derived features.

5. **Data Reduction:**
    - **Feature Selection:** Identify and retain the most relevant features for analysis, using techniques like correlation analysis, feature importance, and recursive feature elimination (RFE).
    - **Dimensionality Reduction:** Reduce the number of features using techniques like Principal Component Analysis (PCA) and Linear Discriminant Analysis (LDA) to simplify the dataset while preserving essential information.

CONCLUSION

Chapter 3 covers the essential steps involved in data collection and preprocessing, including understanding the types of data and sources, data collection methods, and the processes of data cleaning and preparation. By mastering these techniques, you will be able to ensure the quality and accuracy of your data, setting a solid foundation for meaningful analysis and insights.

CHAPTER 4: EXPLORATORY DATA ANALYSIS (EDA)

Understanding Data Through Visualization

Exploratory Data Analysis (EDA) is a critical step in the data science process, aimed at understanding the underlying structure of the data, identifying patterns, and uncovering insights before applying more complex analyses. Visualization is a key component of EDA, as it helps to quickly grasp data distributions, relationships, and anomalies. Common visualization techniques used in EDA include:

- **Histograms:** Used to visualize the distribution of a single numerical variable by dividing the data into bins and plotting the frequency of observations in each bin.
- **Box Plots:** Provide a summary of the distribution of a numerical variable, highlighting the median, quartiles, and potential outliers.
- **Scatter Plots:** Show the relationship between two numerical variables, with each point representing an observation. They are useful for identifying correlations and trends.
- **Pair Plots:** Display scatter plots for pairs of variables in a dataset, helping to visualize relationships and potential interactions among multiple variables.

- **Bar Charts:** Visualize the frequency or proportion of categorical data, making it easy to compare different categories.
- **Heatmaps:** Represent data values in a matrix format using color gradients, useful for visualizing correlations and patterns in large datasets.

Descriptive Statistics

Descriptive statistics summarize and describe the main features of a dataset, providing a simple overview of the data. Key descriptive statistics include:

- **Measures of Central Tendency:**
    - **Mean:** The average value of a numerical variable.
    - **Median:** The middle value when the data is sorted in ascending order.
    - **Mode:** The most frequently occurring value in a dataset.
- **Measures of Dispersion:**
    - **Range:** The difference between the maximum and minimum values.
    - **Variance:** The average squared deviation of each data point from the mean.
    - **Standard Deviation:** The square root of the variance, indicating the spread of data around the mean.
    - **Interquartile Range (IQR):** The range between the first quartile (Q1) and the third quartile (Q3), representing the middle 50% of the data.
- **Shape of Distribution:**
    - **Skewness:** A measure of the asymmetry of the data distribution. Positive skewness indicates a right-skewed distribution, while negative skewness indicates a left-skewed distribution.

- **Kurtosis:** A measure of the "tailedness" of the data distribution. High kurtosis indicates heavy tails, while low kurtosis indicates light tails.

Detecting Patterns and Relationships

EDA involves detecting patterns and relationships within the data to generate hypotheses and guide further analysis. Key techniques include:

- **Correlation Analysis:**
    - **Pearson Correlation Coefficient:** Measures the linear relationship between two numerical variables, ranging from -1 to 1. A value close to 1 indicates a strong positive correlation, while a value close to -1 indicates a strong negative correlation.
    - **Spearman Rank Correlation:** Measures the monotonic relationship between two variables, suitable for ordinal data or non-linear relationships.
    - **Heatmaps:** Visualize correlation matrices to identify pairs of variables with strong relationships.
- **Trend Analysis:**
    - **Time Series Plots:** Visualize data points over time to identify trends, seasonality, and cycles.
    - **Moving Averages:** Smooth out short-term fluctuations to highlight long-term trends.
- **Grouping and Aggregation:**
    - **Group By Operations:** Aggregate data based on categorical variables to compute summary statistics, such as mean, sum, and count, for each group.
    - **Pivot Tables:** Organize and summarize data in a tabular format, allowing for easy comparison of

different groups and categories.

EDA Techniques and Tools

EDA involves a variety of techniques and tools to explore and analyze data effectively. Key techniques include:

- **Data Visualization Tools:**
    - **Matplotlib and Seaborn (Python):** Libraries for creating static, interactive, and animated visualizations in Python.
    - **ggplot2 (R):** A data visualization package in R based on the Grammar of Graphics, allowing users to create complex visualizations with ease.
    - **Tableau:** A leading data visualization tool that enables users to create interactive and shareable dashboards.
- **Statistical Analysis Tools:**
    - **SciPy (Python):** A library for scientific and technical computing, providing functions for statistical analysis, optimization, and signal processing.
    - **Statsmodels (Python):** A library for statistical modeling and hypothesis testing in Python.
    - **R (R Programming Language):** R is known for its strong statistical capabilities, with numerous packages for statistical analysis and modeling.
- **Data Manipulation Tools:**
    - **pandas (Python):** A powerful library for data manipulation and analysis, offering data structures like DataFrame, which allows for efficient handling of large datasets.
    - **dplyr (R):** An essential package in R for data manipulation, providing intuitive functions for filtering, selecting, and transforming data.

CONCLUSION

Chapter 4 covers the essential aspects of Exploratory Data Analysis (EDA), including understanding data through visualization, descriptive statistics, detecting patterns and relationships, and the techniques and tools used in EDA. By mastering EDA, you will be able to uncover valuable insights from your data, generate hypotheses, and lay the groundwork for more advanced analyses.

CHAPTER 5: STATISTICAL ANALYSIS FOR DATA SCIENCE

Probability Theory and Distributions

Probability theory is the mathematical foundation of statistical analysis, providing a framework for quantifying uncertainty and making predictions about random events. Understanding probability and distributions is essential for data science, as it helps in modeling and interpreting data.

- **Basic Probability Concepts:**
    - **Experiment:** A procedure that generates a set of outcomes.
    - **Sample Space:** The set of all possible outcomes of an experiment.
    - **Event:** A subset of the sample space.
    - **Probability:** A measure of the likelihood of an event occurring, ranging from 0 (impossible) to 1 (certain).
- **Probability Rules:**
    - **Addition Rule:** The probability of the union of two events.
    - **Multiplication Rule:** The probability of the intersection of two events.
    - **Conditional Probability:** The probability of an

event given that another event has occurred.
- **Bayes' Theorem:** A formula that relates conditional probabilities and allows for updating probabilities based on new information.
- **Probability Distributions:**
  - **Discrete Distributions:** Distributions for discrete random variables, such as the Binomial, Poisson, and Geometric distributions.
  - **Continuous Distributions:** Distributions for continuous random variables, such as the Normal (Gaussian), Exponential, and Uniform distributions.

Hypothesis Testing

Hypothesis testing is a statistical method used to make inferences about populations based on sample data. It involves formulating a hypothesis, collecting data, and determining whether the data supports or rejects the hypothesis.

- **Steps in Hypothesis Testing:**
  - **Formulate Hypotheses:** Define the null hypothesis (H0) and the alternative hypothesis (H1).
  - **Choose a Significance Level:** Determine the significance level (alpha), typically set at 0.05.
  - **Select a Test Statistic:** Choose the appropriate test statistic based on the data and hypothesis.
  - **Calculate the Test Statistic and P-value:** Compute the test statistic and the corresponding p-value.
  - **Decision Rule:** Compare the p-value to the significance level and make a decision to reject or fail to reject the null hypothesis.
- **Common Hypothesis Tests:**

- **Z-Test:** Used for comparing means when the population variance is known.
- **T-Test:** Used for comparing means when the population variance is unknown. Includes one-sample, two-sample, and paired t-tests.
- **Chi-Square Test:** Used for testing relationships between categorical variables.
- **ANOVA (Analysis of Variance):** Used for comparing means across multiple groups.

Regression Analysis

Regression analysis is a statistical technique used to model the relationship between a dependent variable and one or more independent variables. It is widely used for prediction and forecasting.

- **Linear Regression:**
  - **Simple Linear Regression:** Models the relationship between two variables using a linear equation: $y = \beta_0 + \beta_1 x + \epsilon$.
  - **Multiple Linear Regression:** Extends simple linear regression to include multiple independent variables: $y = \beta_0 + \beta_1 x_1 + \beta_2 x_2 + \ldots + \beta_n x_n + \epsilon$.
- **Model Evaluation:**
  - **R-squared (R^2):** A measure of the proportion of variance in the dependent variable explained by the independent variables.
  - **Adjusted R-squared:** Adjusts the R-squared value for the number of predictors in the model.
  - **P-values:** Indicate the significance of individual predictors.
  - **Residual Analysis:** Examines the differences

between observed and predicted values to assess model fit.
- **Assumptions of Linear Regression:**
    - **Linearity:** The relationship between independent and dependent variables is linear.
    - **Independence:** Observations are independent of each other.
    - **Homoscedasticity:** The variance of residuals is constant across all levels of the independent variables.
    - **Normality:** Residuals are normally distributed.

Bayesian Statistics

Bayesian statistics is an approach to statistical inference that incorporates prior knowledge or beliefs along with the observed data to make probabilistic statements about parameters.

- **Bayesian Inference:**
    - **Prior Distribution:** Represents the initial belief about a parameter before observing the data.
    - **Likelihood Function:** Represents the probability of the observed data given the parameter.
    - **Posterior Distribution:** Combines the prior distribution and likelihood function to update the belief about the parameter after observing the data.
- **Bayes' Theorem:** The mathematical foundation of Bayesian inference:

$$P(\theta | D) = \frac{P(D | \theta) \cdot P(\theta)}{P(D)}$$

where $P(\theta | D)$ is the posterior distribution, $P(D | \theta)$ is the likelihood, $P(\theta)$ is the prior distribution, and $P(D)$ is the marginal likelihood.

- **Applications of Bayesian Statistics:**

- **Parameter Estimation:** Estimating the parameters of a probability distribution.
- **Model Comparison:** Comparing different models using Bayesian criteria.
- **Predictive Modeling:** Making predictions based on the posterior distribution.

CONCLUSION

Chapter 5 delves into the fundamental concepts of statistical analysis for data science, including probability theory, hypothesis testing, regression analysis, and Bayesian statistics. By mastering these statistical techniques, you will be equipped to analyze data, draw meaningful conclusions, and make informed decisions based on data-driven insights.

CHAPTER 6: INTRODUCTION TO MACHINE LEARNING

Supervised vs. Unsupervised Learning

Machine learning is a core component of data science, involving the development of algorithms that enable computers to learn from data and make predictions or decisions without explicit programming. There are two primary types of machine learning: supervised and unsupervised learning.

- **Supervised Learning:**
    - In supervised learning, the algorithm is trained on a labeled dataset, where the input data is paired with the correct output. The goal is to learn a mapping from inputs to outputs and make accurate predictions on new, unseen data.
    - **Examples:**
        - Classification: Predicting the category or class of an instance (e.g., spam detection in emails).
        - Regression: Predicting a continuous value (e.g., predicting house prices).
- **Unsupervised Learning:**
    - In unsupervised learning, the algorithm is trained on an unlabeled dataset, where the input

data does not have corresponding output labels. The goal is to identify patterns, structures, or relationships within the data.
- **Examples:**
  - Clustering: Grouping similar instances together (e.g., customer segmentation).
  - Dimensionality Reduction: Reducing the number of features while preserving important information (e.g., Principal Component Analysis).

Key Algorithms and Techniques

Machine learning involves a wide range of algorithms and techniques, each suitable for different types of problems and datasets. Key algorithms include:

- **Linear Regression:** A simple algorithm used for regression tasks, modeling the relationship between a dependent variable and one or more independent variables with a linear equation.
- **Logistic Regression:** Used for binary classification tasks, modeling the probability that an instance belongs to a particular class.
- **Decision Trees:** A tree-based algorithm used for both classification and regression, where each node represents a decision based on a feature, and each leaf represents an outcome.
- **Random Forests:** An ensemble learning method that combines multiple decision trees to improve accuracy and reduce overfitting.
- **Support Vector Machines (SVM):** A powerful algorithm for classification tasks that finds the optimal hyperplane to separate different classes in the feature space.
- **K-Nearest Neighbors (KNN):** A simple, instance-based algorithm used for both classification and regression,

where predictions are based on the majority class or average value of the nearest neighbors.
- **K-Means Clustering:** A popular clustering algorithm that partitions the data into K clusters, minimizing the within-cluster variance.
- **Principal Component Analysis (PCA):** A dimensionality reduction technique that transforms the data into a lower-dimensional space while preserving the most important information.

Model Training and Evaluation

The process of training a machine learning model involves several steps:

1. **Data Preparation:**
   - **Feature Selection:** Identify and select relevant features for the model.
   - **Data Splitting:** Split the dataset into training and test sets to evaluate the model's performance on unseen data.
2. **Training the Model:**
   - **Algorithm Selection:** Choose an appropriate algorithm based on the problem and data characteristics.
   - **Model Training:** Fit the model to the training data by adjusting its parameters to minimize the error or maximize the accuracy.
3. **Model Evaluation:**
   - **Performance Metrics:** Use various metrics to evaluate the model's performance, such as accuracy, precision, recall, F1-score, and mean squared error (MSE).
   - **Cross-Validation:** Split the data into multiple folds and train the model on different subsets to ensure robustness and avoid overfitting.

- **Confusion Matrix:** For classification tasks, use a confusion matrix to visualize the performance, showing true positives, true negatives, false positives, and false negatives.

Overfitting and Underfitting

Overfitting and underfitting are common challenges in machine learning, impacting the model's ability to generalize to new data.

- **Overfitting:**
  - Occurs when a model learns the noise and details of the training data too well, resulting in high accuracy on the training set but poor performance on the test set. Overfitting can be mitigated by:
    - Using simpler models with fewer parameters.
    - Implementing regularization techniques (e.g., L1, L2 regularization).
    - Using cross-validation to tune hyperparameters.
    - Increasing the size of the training dataset.
- **Underfitting:**
  - Occurs when a model is too simple to capture the underlying patterns in the data, resulting in poor performance on both the training and test sets. Underfitting can be addressed by:
    - Using more complex models with additional features.
    - Increasing the model's capacity (e.g., more layers in a neural network).
    - Reducing regularization.
    - Ensuring proper feature engineering and selection.

CONCLUSION

Chapter 6 introduces the fundamental concepts of machine learning, including the differences between supervised and unsupervised learning, key algorithms and techniques, the process of model training and evaluation, and the challenges of overfitting and underfitting. By understanding these core principles, you will be equipped to build and evaluate effective machine learning models, paving the way for more advanced techniques in subsequent chapters.

CHAPTER 7: SUPERVISED LEARNING ALGORITHMS

Linear Regression

Linear regression is a fundamental algorithm used for regression tasks, where the goal is to predict a continuous target variable based on one or more input features. It models the relationship between the dependent variable (target) and independent variables (features) using a linear equation:

$$y = \beta_0 + \beta_1 x_1 + \beta_2 x_2 + \ldots + \beta_n x_n + \epsilon$$

- **Simple Linear Regression:** Involves a single feature and models the relationship between two variables.
- **Multiple Linear Regression:** Involves multiple features and models the relationship between the target variable and several predictors.

Key Concepts:
- **Coefficients (β):** Represent the slope of the line and quantify the relationship between each feature and the target variable.
- **Intercept (β_0):** Represents the value of the target variable when all features are zero.

- **Residuals (ε):** The differences between the observed and predicted values of the target variable.

Logistic Regression

Logistic regression is used for binary classification tasks, where the goal is to predict a binary outcome (0 or 1) based on one or more input features. Unlike linear regression, logistic regression models the probability of the target variable using the logistic function:

$$P(y=1|x) = \frac{1}{1 + e^{-(\beta_0 + \beta_1 x_1 + \beta_2 x_2 + \ldots + \beta_n x_n)}}$$

- **Binary Classification:** Predicts whether an instance belongs to one of two classes.
- **Multinomial Logistic Regression:** Extends logistic regression to handle multiple classes.

Key Concepts:

- **Odds Ratio:** The ratio of the probability of an event occurring to the probability of it not occurring.
- **Logit Function:** The natural logarithm of the odds ratio.
- **Decision Boundary:** The threshold used to classify instances based on predicted probabilities.

Decision Trees

Decision trees are versatile algorithms used for both classification and regression tasks. They model decisions and their possible consequences in a tree-like structure, where each node represents a decision based on a feature, and each leaf node represents an outcome.

- **Classification Trees:** Predict categorical outcomes by splitting the data based on feature values.
- **Regression Trees:** Predict continuous outcomes by partitioning the data into subsets and fitting a simple model (e.g., mean) to each subset.

Key Concepts:

- **Gini Impurity:** A measure of the impurity or diversity of a dataset. Used to determine the best split in a classification tree.
- **Entropy:** Another measure of impurity, based on information theory. Used in algorithms like ID3.
- **Information Gain:** The reduction in entropy achieved by splitting the data based on a feature.
- **Pruning:** The process of removing nodes to reduce overfitting and improve generalization.

Random Forests

Random forests are ensemble learning methods that combine multiple decision trees to improve accuracy and reduce overfitting. They work by training multiple trees on different subsets of the data and averaging their predictions.

- **Bagging:** Bootstrap aggregating, a technique where multiple subsets of the data are randomly sampled with replacement to train individual trees.
- **Feature Randomness:** Each tree is trained using a random subset of features, increasing diversity among the trees.

Key Concepts:

- **Voting (Classification):** The final prediction is based on the majority vote of all the trees.
- **Averaging (Regression):** The final prediction is the average of the predictions from all the trees.
- **Feature Importance:** The importance of each feature in making predictions, determined by averaging the decrease in impurity across all trees.

Support Vector Machines (SVM)

Support Vector Machines (SVM) are powerful algorithms used for classification tasks. They work by finding the optimal hyperplane that separates different classes in the feature space with the maximum margin.

- **Linear SVM:** Finds a linear hyperplane to separate the classes.
- **Kernel SVM:** Uses kernel functions to transform the data into a higher-dimensional space, making it possible to find non-linear decision boundaries.

Key Concepts:

- **Support Vectors:** The data points closest to the hyperplane, which influence its position and orientation.
- **Margin:** The distance between the hyperplane and the nearest support vectors. SVM aims to maximize this margin.
- **Kernel Trick:** A technique that allows SVM to operate in a high-dimensional space without explicitly computing the coordinates, using functions like polynomial, radial basis function (RBF), and sigmoid kernels.

CONCLUSION

Chapter 7 explores various supervised learning algorithms, including linear regression, logistic regression, decision trees, random forests, and support vector machines (SVM). By understanding these algorithms and their key concepts, you will be equipped to handle a wide range of classification and regression tasks, making accurate predictions and driving data-driven decisions.

CHAPTER 8: UNSUPERVISED LEARNING ALGORITHMS

Clustering Techniques

Clustering is an unsupervised learning technique used to group similar data points into clusters based on their characteristics. It helps identify patterns and structures within the data without predefined labels. Key clustering algorithms include:

- **K-Means Clustering:**
    - **Overview:** K-means clustering partitions the data into K clusters, where each data point belongs to the cluster with the nearest mean.
    - **Algorithm Steps:**
        1. Initialize K centroids randomly.
        2. Assign each data point to the nearest centroid.
        3. Update the centroids by calculating the mean of the assigned points.
        4. Repeat steps 2 and 3 until the centroids converge.
    - **Choosing K:** The number of clusters (K) can

be determined using methods like the Elbow Method or Silhouette Analysis.
- **Hierarchical Clustering:**
    - **Overview:** Hierarchical clustering creates a tree-like structure (dendrogram) to represent the nested grouping of data points.
    - **Types:**
        - **Agglomerative Clustering:** Starts with each data point as a separate cluster and merges the closest pairs of clusters iteratively until all points are in a single cluster.
        - **Divisive Clustering:** Starts with all data points in a single cluster and recursively splits them into smaller clusters.
    - **Distance Metrics:** Common distance metrics include Euclidean distance, Manhattan distance, and cosine similarity.
    - **Linkage Criteria:** Methods for measuring the distance between clusters include single linkage, complete linkage, and average linkage.

Principal Component Analysis (PCA)

Principal Component Analysis (PCA) is a dimensionality reduction technique used to transform high-dimensional data into a lower-dimensional space while preserving the most important information.

- **Overview:**
    - PCA identifies the principal components (orthogonal vectors) that capture the maximum variance in the data.
    - These components are linear combinations of the original features.
- **Algorithm Steps:**

1. Standardize the data to have zero mean and unit variance.
2. Compute the covariance matrix of the standardized data.
3. Perform eigenvalue decomposition on the covariance matrix to obtain eigenvalues and eigenvectors.
4. Select the top principal components based on the largest eigenvalues.
5. Project the data onto the selected principal components to obtain the reduced-dimensional representation.

- **Applications:**
  - PCA is used for noise reduction, feature extraction, and data visualization in high-dimensional datasets.

Anomaly Detection

Anomaly detection is an unsupervised learning technique used to identify rare or abnormal instances that deviate significantly from the majority of the data.

- **Techniques:**
  - **Statistical Methods:** Assume a statistical distribution for the data and flag instances that fall outside the expected range.
  - **Distance-Based Methods:** Measure the distance between data points and identify outliers based on their distance from the majority of points (e.g., K-nearest neighbors).
  - **Density-Based Methods:** Identify anomalies based on the density of data points in the feature space (e.g., DBSCAN, Isolation Forest).
- **Applications:**
  - Anomaly detection is used in fraud detection,

network security, industrial monitoring, and fault detection.

Association Rule Learning

Association rule learning is an unsupervised learning technique used to discover interesting relationships or associations between variables in large datasets.

- **Apriori Algorithm:**
    - **Overview:** The Apriori algorithm identifies frequent itemsets (combinations of items) and generates association rules based on these itemsets.
    - **Algorithm Steps:**
        1. Identify frequent itemsets that satisfy a minimum support threshold.
        2. Generate association rules from these itemsets that satisfy a minimum confidence threshold.
- **Metrics:**
    - **Support:** The proportion of transactions that contain a specific itemset.
    - **Confidence:** The likelihood that a transaction containing a specific itemset also contains another itemset.
    - **Lift:** The ratio of the observed support to the expected support if the itemsets were independent.
- **Applications:**
    - Association rule learning is widely used in market basket analysis, recommendation systems, and cross-selling strategies.

CONCLUSION

Chapter 8 explores various unsupervised learning algorithms, including clustering techniques like K-means and hierarchical clustering, dimensionality reduction with Principal Component Analysis (PCA), anomaly detection methods, and association rule learning. By understanding these algorithms and their key concepts, you will be equipped to uncover hidden patterns and structures within your data, enabling you to gain valuable insights and make informed decisions.

CHAPTER 9: ADVANCED MACHINE LEARNING TECHNIQUES

Ensemble Learning

Ensemble learning involves combining multiple machine learning models to improve overall performance and robustness compared to individual models. The key idea is that a group of weak learners can come together to form a strong learner. Major ensemble techniques include:

- **Bagging (Bootstrap Aggregating):**
  - **Overview:** Bagging involves training multiple instances of the same model on different subsets of the training data, generated through random sampling with replacement.
  - **Example:** Random Forest, which combines multiple decision trees to improve accuracy and reduce overfitting.
- **Boosting:**
  - **Overview:** Boosting sequentially trains a series of weak learners, each focusing on correcting the errors of its predecessor.
  - **Examples:**

- **AdaBoost (Adaptive Boosting):** Adjusts the weights of incorrectly classified instances, allowing subsequent models to focus on these harder cases.
- **Gradient Boosting:** Builds each new model to predict the residual errors of the previous models, improving overall accuracy.

- **Stacking:**
  - **Overview:** Stacking involves training multiple base models and then using a meta-model to combine their predictions.
  - **Process:** The base models are trained on the training data, and their predictions serve as inputs for the meta-model, which is trained to produce the final prediction.

Gradient Boosting Machines

Gradient Boosting Machines (GBM) are powerful ensemble techniques used for regression and classification tasks. They build models sequentially, with each new model correcting the errors of its predecessors.

- **Key Concepts:**
  - **Boosting:** Each model in the sequence is trained to predict the residual errors of the previous models.
  - **Learning Rate:** A parameter that controls the contribution of each model to the final prediction, helping to prevent overfitting.
  - **Tree Depth:** Limits the complexity of individual trees in the ensemble, balancing bias and variance.
- **Popular Implementations:**
  - **XGBoost (Extreme Gradient Boosting):** An

efficient and scalable implementation of gradient boosting, widely used in machine learning competitions.
- **LightGBM (Light Gradient Boosting Machine):** Optimized for speed and performance, particularly with large datasets.
- **CatBoost:** Handles categorical features natively and is designed to minimize overfitting and improve accuracy.

Neural Networks and Deep Learning

Neural networks are a class of machine learning models inspired by the structure and function of the human brain. They consist of interconnected layers of neurons that process and learn from data. Deep learning involves training deep neural networks with many layers, allowing them to capture complex patterns and representations.

- **Key Components:**
    - **Neurons:** Basic units that perform computations, passing signals through activation functions.
    - **Layers:** Organized groups of neurons, including input, hidden, and output layers.
    - **Weights and Biases:** Parameters that are adjusted during training to minimize the error between predicted and actual values.
    - **Activation Functions:** Non-linear functions applied to neuron outputs, enabling neural networks to capture complex patterns (e.g., ReLU, Sigmoid, Tanh).
- **Training Process:**
    - **Forward Propagation:** Computes the output of the network by passing the input through each layer.

- **Loss Function:** Measures the error between the predicted output and the actual target.
- **Backpropagation:** Adjusts the weights and biases by propagating the error backward through the network, using gradient descent to minimize the loss.

- Common Architectures:
    - **Feedforward Neural Networks:** Simple neural networks where connections do not form cycles.
    - **Convolutional Neural Networks (CNNs):** Specialized for processing grid-like data, such as images, using convolutional layers to capture spatial hierarchies.
    - **Recurrent Neural Networks (RNNs):** Designed for sequential data, such as time series or text, with connections forming directed cycles to capture temporal dependencies.
    - **Generative Adversarial Networks (GANs):** Consist of two networks—a generator and a discriminator—that compete to produce realistic synthetic data.

Natural Language Processing (NLP)

Natural Language Processing (NLP) involves the interaction between computers and human language, enabling machines to understand, interpret, and generate text. Key NLP techniques include:

- Text Preprocessing:
    - **Tokenization:** Splitting text into individual words or tokens.
    - **Stop Words Removal:** Eliminating common words that do not carry significant meaning (e.g., "the", "and").
    - **Stemming and Lemmatization:** Reducing

words to their base or root forms.
- **Vectorization:** Converting text into numerical representations, such as Term Frequency-Inverse Document Frequency (TF-IDF) and word embeddings (e.g., Word2Vec, GloVe).

- **Text Classification:**
  - **Sentiment Analysis:** Determining the sentiment or emotion expressed in text (e.g., positive, negative, neutral).
  - **Topic Modeling:** Identifying the main topics or themes within a collection of documents (e.g., Latent Dirichlet Allocation (LDA)).
  - **Named Entity Recognition (NER):** Detecting and classifying named entities (e.g., people, organizations, locations) in text.

- **Advanced NLP Techniques:**
  - **Recurrent Neural Networks (RNNs):** Capturing temporal dependencies in sequential data, with architectures like Long Short-Term Memory (LSTM) and Gated Recurrent Unit (GRU).
  - **Transformers:** State-of-the-art models for NLP tasks, using self-attention mechanisms to capture long-range dependencies (e.g., BERT, GPT).

CONCLUSION

Chapter 9 explores advanced machine learning techniques, including ensemble learning, gradient boosting machines, neural networks, deep learning, and natural language processing (NLP). By understanding these sophisticated algorithms and their applications, you will be equipped to tackle complex data science problems and leverage cutting-edge technologies to extract valuable insights from data.

CHAPTER 10: MODEL EVALUATION AND OPTIMIZATION

Metrics for Model Evaluation

Evaluating the performance of machine learning models is crucial to ensure they meet the desired criteria and perform well on new, unseen data. Various metrics are used depending on the type of problem, such as classification or regression.

- **Classification Metrics:**
    - **Accuracy:** The ratio of correctly predicted instances to the total instances. It is a simple metric but can be misleading in imbalanced datasets.
    - **Precision:** The ratio of true positive predictions to the total predicted positives. It measures the accuracy of positive predictions.
    - **Recall (Sensitivity):** The ratio of true positive predictions to the total actual positives. It measures the model's ability to detect positive instances.
    - **F1-Score:** The harmonic mean of precision and recall, providing a balance between the two. It is useful when dealing with imbalanced classes.
    - **Confusion Matrix:** A table that shows the true

positives, true negatives, false positives, and false negatives, providing a comprehensive view of the model's performance.
  - **ROC Curve and AUC:** The Receiver Operating Characteristic (ROC) curve plots the true positive rate against the false positive rate, and the Area Under the Curve (AUC) measures the overall performance.
- **Regression Metrics:**
  - **Mean Absolute Error (MAE):** The average of the absolute differences between the predicted and actual values.
  - **Mean Squared Error (MSE):** The average of the squared differences between the predicted and actual values, penalizing larger errors more.
  - **Root Mean Squared Error (RMSE):** The square root of the MSE, providing an error metric in the same units as the target variable.
  - **R-squared (R^2):** The proportion of variance in the target variable explained by the model. It ranges from 0 to 1, with higher values indicating better performance.
  - **Adjusted R-squared:** Adjusted for the number of predictors in the model, providing a more accurate measure of model fit.

Cross-Validation Techniques

Cross-validation is a technique used to assess the generalizability of a machine learning model by evaluating its performance on different subsets of the data. It helps prevent overfitting and provides a more reliable estimate of model performance.

- **K-Fold Cross-Validation:**
  - **Overview:** The dataset is split into K equal-sized folds. The model is trained on K-1 folds and

tested on the remaining fold. This process is repeated K times, with each fold serving as the test set once.
  - **Advantages:** Provides a robust estimate of model performance and helps in identifying variance in the model's predictions.
- **Leave-One-Out Cross-Validation (LOOCV):**
  - **Overview:** A special case of K-fold cross-validation where K is equal to the number of instances in the dataset. Each instance is used as a test set once, and the model is trained on the remaining data.
  - **Advantages:** Provides a thorough evaluation of model performance but can be computationally expensive for large datasets.
- **Stratified Cross-Validation:**
  - **Overview:** Ensures that each fold in cross-validation has a similar distribution of the target variable, particularly useful for imbalanced datasets.
  - **Advantages:** Provides a more representative evaluation of model performance in datasets with class imbalance.

Hyperparameter Tuning

Hyperparameter tuning involves optimizing the hyperparameters of a machine learning model to improve its performance. Hyperparameters are settings that control the behavior of the model and are not learned from the data.

- **Grid Search:**
  - **Overview:** Exhaustively searches through a predefined set of hyperparameters to identify the best combination based on model performance.

- **Advantages:** Simple to implement and guarantees finding the optimal combination within the specified grid.
- **Random Search:**
  - **Overview:** Randomly samples hyperparameter values from a predefined distribution, exploring a wider range of values compared to grid search.
  - **Advantages:** Often more efficient than grid search and can find good hyperparameter combinations with fewer iterations.
- **Bayesian Optimization:**
  - **Overview:** Uses probabilistic models to predict the performance of different hyperparameter combinations and iteratively updates the search based on these predictions.
  - **Advantages:** More efficient than grid and random search, often leading to better hyperparameter settings with fewer evaluations.

Model Selection and Comparison

Selecting the best model and comparing different models are essential steps in the machine learning workflow. Key techniques include:

- **Validation Curves:**
  - **Overview:** Plot the model's performance metric as a function of a hyperparameter, helping identify the optimal value for that hyperparameter.
  - **Advantages:** Visualizes the impact of hyperparameters on model performance, aiding in hyperparameter tuning.
- **Learning Curves:**
  - **Overview:** Plot the model's performance on the

training and validation sets as a function of the number of training instances.
- **Advantages:** Helps diagnose issues like overfitting and underfitting by showing how the model's performance changes with more data.

- **Model Comparison:**
    - **Overview:** Use cross-validation and statistical tests to compare the performance of different models, selecting the best one based on relevant metrics.
    - **Advantages:** Ensures that the chosen model is not only accurate but also generalizes well to new data.

CONCLUSION

Chapter 10 covers essential techniques for evaluating and optimizing machine learning models, including various performance metrics, cross-validation methods, hyperparameter tuning, and model selection. By mastering these techniques, you will be able to build robust and reliable models that perform well on unseen data, ensuring accurate and meaningful predictions.

CHAPTER 11: BIG DATA AND DATA ENGINEERING

Introduction to Big Data

Big data refers to the vast volumes of data generated by various sources at high velocity and in a variety of formats. The three Vs of big data – volume, velocity, and variety – distinguish it from traditional data and require specialized tools and techniques for storage, processing, and analysis.

- **Volume:** The sheer amount of data generated from multiple sources, such as social media, sensors, transactions, and more.
- **Velocity:** The speed at which data is generated, collected, and processed. Real-time or near-real-time data processing is often required.
- **Variety:** The different types of data, including structured, unstructured, and semi-structured data, such as text, images, videos, and logs.

Big Data Technologies

Several technologies and frameworks are designed to handle big data, providing efficient storage, processing, and analysis capabilities.

- **Hadoop:**
  - **Overview:** An open-source framework that

allows for distributed storage and processing of large datasets across clusters of computers.
- **Components:**
  - **Hadoop Distributed File System (HDFS):** Provides scalable and reliable storage.
  - **MapReduce:** A programming model for processing large datasets in parallel.
  - **YARN (Yet Another Resource Negotiator):** Manages and schedules resources for various applications.

- **Apache Spark:**
  - **Overview:** A fast, in-memory data processing engine that provides a wide range of capabilities, including batch processing, real-time streaming, machine learning, and graph processing.
  - **Components:**
    - **Spark Core:** The foundation for all Spark functionalities.
    - **Spark SQL:** Enables querying structured data using SQL and DataFrame APIs.
    - **Spark Streaming:** Processes real-time data streams.
    - **MLlib:** A library for scalable machine learning.
    - **GraphX:** A library for graph processing.

- **Apache Kafka:**
  - **Overview:** A distributed streaming platform that allows for real-time data ingestion, processing, and analysis.
  - **Components:**
    - **Producer:** Publishes data to Kafka topics.

- **Consumer:** Subscribes to Kafka topics and processes the data.
- **Broker:** Manages the storage and retrieval of data in Kafka.
- **ZooKeeper:** Coordinates and manages Kafka brokers.

Data Warehousing and ETL Processes

Data warehousing involves storing and managing large volumes of structured data for reporting and analysis. ETL (Extract, Transform, Load) processes are used to move data from various sources into the data warehouse.

- **Data Warehousing:**
    - **Overview:** Centralized repositories that store structured data from multiple sources, designed for query and analysis.
    - **Key Technologies:**
        - **Amazon Redshift:** A cloud-based data warehouse service.
        - **Google BigQuery:** A fully-managed, serverless data warehouse service.
        - **Snowflake:** A cloud-native data warehousing solution.
- **ETL Processes:**
    - **Extract:** Collecting data from various sources, such as databases, APIs, and files.
    - **Transform:** Cleaning, formatting, and transforming data into a consistent format suitable for analysis.
    - **Load:** Storing the transformed data into the data warehouse for querying and analysis.
- **ETL Tools:**
    - **Apache NiFi:** An open-source tool for

automating data flow between systems.
- **Talend:** A data integration platform that provides ETL capabilities.
- **Informatica:** A data management and integration platform for ETL processes.

Scalable Data Pipelines

Scalable data pipelines are essential for efficiently processing and analyzing large volumes of data. Key components of scalable data pipelines include:

- **Data Ingestion:**
  - **Real-Time Ingestion:** Tools like Apache Kafka and Amazon Kinesis enable real-time data ingestion.
  - **Batch Ingestion:** Tools like Apache Sqoop and AWS Data Pipeline enable batch data ingestion from various sources.
- **Data Processing:**
  - **Stream Processing:** Tools like Apache Flink and Apache Storm process data streams in real-time.
  - **Batch Processing:** Tools like Apache Hadoop and Apache Spark process large datasets in batches.
- **Data Storage:**
  - **Data Lakes:** Centralized repositories that store raw and unprocessed data, allowing for flexible analysis and processing.
    - **Examples:** Amazon S3, Azure Data Lake Storage, Google Cloud Storage.
  - **Data Warehouses:** Structured storage for processed data, optimized for querying and analysis.
- **Workflow Orchestration:**
  - **Apache Airflow:** An open-source tool for

designing, scheduling, and monitoring data workflows.
- **Prefect:** A data workflow automation tool that enables orchestrating complex data pipelines.

CONCLUSION

Chapter 11 explores the essential concepts and technologies of big data and data engineering, including big data technologies like Hadoop and Spark, data warehousing and ETL processes, and scalable data pipelines. By understanding these components, you will be equipped to handle large-scale data processing and analysis, enabling you to extract valuable insights from big data.

CHAPTER 12: TIME SERIES ANALYSIS AND FORECASTING

Understanding Time Series Data

Time series data is a sequence of data points collected or recorded at specific time intervals. Unlike other types of data, time series data has a temporal ordering, meaning the order of the data points is significant. Examples of time series data include stock prices, temperature readings, sales figures, and website traffic.

Key characteristics of time series data:

- **Trend:** The long-term upward or downward movement in the data.
- **Seasonality:** Regular, repeating patterns or cycles within the data, such as daily, weekly, monthly, or yearly cycles.
- **Noise:** Random variability in the data that cannot be attributed to trends or seasonality.
- **Stationarity:** A property of time series data where the statistical properties (mean, variance, etc.) remain constant over time. Non-stationary data exhibits trends, seasonality, or changing variance.

Decomposition and Smoothing

Decomposition is the process of breaking down a time series into its constituent components: trend, seasonality, and residuals (noise). This helps in understanding the underlying patterns and making more accurate forecasts.

- **Additive Decomposition:** Assumes the time series is the sum of its components.

$y_t = T_t + S_t + e_t$

- **Multiplicative Decomposition:** Assumes the time series is the product of its components.

$y_t = T_t \times S_t \times e_t$

Smoothing techniques are used to remove noise and highlight patterns in the data.

- **Moving Averages:** Calculate the average of a fixed number of consecutive data points to smooth the time series.
    - **Simple Moving Average (SMA):** Averages a fixed number of past observations.
    - **Exponential Moving Average (EMA):** Gives more weight to recent observations, making it more responsive to changes.
- **LOESS (Locally Estimated Scatterplot Smoothing):** A non-parametric method that fits multiple regression models to localized subsets of the data.

ARIMA Models

AutoRegressive Integrated Moving Average (ARIMA) models are widely used for time series forecasting. They combine three components:

- **Autoregression (AR):** Models the relationship between a current observation and a number of past observations.
- **Integration (I):** Represents the differencing of observations to make the time series stationary.
- **Moving Average (MA):** Models the relationship between a current observation and past forecast errors.

The ARIMA model is denoted as ARIMA(p, d, q), where:

- **p:** The number of lag observations included in the model (AR part).
- **d:** The number of times the raw observations are differenced to achieve stationarity (I part).
- **q:** The size of the moving average window (MA part).

Steps to build an ARIMA model:

1. **Stationarity Check:** Use the Augmented Dickey-Fuller (ADF) test to check if the time series is stationary.
2. **Differencing:** Apply differencing if the series is non-stationary.
3. **Determine Parameters:** Use autocorrelation function (ACF) and partial autocorrelation function (PACF) plots to determine the values of p and q.
4. **Model Fitting:** Fit the ARIMA model to the data.
5. **Model Diagnostics:** Check the residuals to ensure they resemble white noise.
6. **Forecasting:** Generate forecasts using the fitted ARIMA model.

Advanced Forecasting Techniques

Beyond ARIMA, there are several advanced techniques for time series forecasting:

- **Seasonal ARIMA (SARIMA):** Extends ARIMA to handle seasonal data by incorporating seasonal components. Denoted as SARIMA(p, d, q)(P, D, Q, m), where P, D, Q, and m represent the seasonal components.
- **Exponential Smoothing (ETS):** Forecasts based on weighted averages of past observations, with recent observations given more weight. Includes simple exponential smoothing, Holt's linear trend model, and Holt-Winters seasonal model.
- **Prophet:** An open-source forecasting tool developed by Facebook, designed for forecasting time series data that

exhibits strong seasonal patterns and historical data.
- **LSTM (Long Short-Term Memory) Networks:** A type of recurrent neural network (RNN) that excels in learning long-term dependencies in sequential data. Effective for complex time series forecasting.

Practical Applications

Time series analysis and forecasting have a wide range of applications across various industries:

- **Finance:** Predicting stock prices, interest rates, and economic indicators.
- **Retail:** Forecasting sales, demand, and inventory levels.
- **Energy:** Predicting energy consumption and production.
- **Weather:** Forecasting temperature, precipitation, and other weather conditions.
- **Healthcare:** Monitoring and predicting disease outbreaks and patient admissions.

CONCLUSION

Chapter 12 covers the essential concepts and techniques of time series analysis and forecasting, including understanding time series data, decomposition and smoothing, ARIMA models, advanced forecasting techniques, and practical applications. By mastering these methods, you will be equipped to analyze and forecast time-dependent data, enabling you to make informed decisions and drive business value.

CHAPTER 13: DATA SCIENCE IN PRACTICE

Case Studies and Real-World Applications

Data science is a versatile field with applications across various industries. By examining real-world case studies, we can understand how data science techniques are applied to solve complex problems and drive business value.

- **Healthcare:**
    - **Predictive Analytics for Patient Outcomes:** Hospitals use machine learning models to predict patient outcomes, such as the likelihood of readmission, enabling proactive care and resource allocation.
    - **Personalized Medicine:** Data science helps in analyzing genetic data to develop personalized treatment plans, improving patient outcomes and reducing side effects.
- **Finance:**
    - **Fraud Detection:** Financial institutions use machine learning algorithms to detect fraudulent transactions in real-time, protecting customers and reducing losses.
    - **Algorithmic Trading:** Data science models analyze market data to make trading decisions, maximizing returns and minimizing risks.

- **Retail:**
  - **Customer Segmentation:** Retailers use clustering algorithms to segment customers based on purchasing behavior, enabling targeted marketing campaigns.
  - **Inventory Management:** Predictive models forecast demand, optimizing inventory levels and reducing stockouts and overstock situations.
- **Transportation:**
  - **Route Optimization:** Logistics companies use optimization algorithms to determine the most efficient routes, reducing fuel consumption and delivery times.
  - **Predictive Maintenance:** Data science models predict equipment failures, allowing for timely maintenance and reducing downtime.
- **Marketing:**
  - **Customer Lifetime Value (CLV) Prediction:** Companies use data science to predict the lifetime value of customers, informing marketing strategies and resource allocation.
  - **Sentiment Analysis:** Analyzing social media data to gauge customer sentiment, helping companies understand brand perception and improve customer experience.

Industry-Specific Use Cases

Data science techniques are tailored to address industry-specific challenges and opportunities. Some notable industry-specific use cases include:

- **Energy:**
  - **Demand Forecasting:** Predicting energy consumption patterns to optimize energy

production and distribution.
- **Smart Grid Management:** Using data analytics to monitor and control the electricity grid, improving efficiency and reliability.

- **Manufacturing:**
  - **Quality Control:** Analyzing production data to identify defects and improve product quality.
  - **Supply Chain Optimization:** Using predictive analytics to manage supply chain risks and ensure timely delivery of raw materials and products.

- **Education:**
  - **Student Performance Prediction:** Predicting student performance and identifying at-risk students, enabling targeted interventions and support.
  - **Curriculum Optimization:** Analyzing student feedback and performance data to optimize curriculum design and delivery.

- **Entertainment:**
  - **Content Recommendation:** Streaming platforms use collaborative filtering and deep learning algorithms to recommend personalized content to users.
  - **Audience Analysis:** Analyzing viewership data to understand audience preferences and optimize content production.

Ethical Considerations in Data Science

While data science offers numerous benefits, it also raises ethical considerations that must be addressed to ensure responsible and fair use of data.

- **Bias and Fairness:**
  - **Understanding Bias:** Identifying and mitigating

biases in data and algorithms to ensure fair and equitable outcomes.
- **Fairness Metrics:** Using fairness metrics to evaluate and improve the fairness of machine learning models.

- **Privacy and Security:**
  - **Data Privacy:** Ensuring that personal data is collected, stored, and used in compliance with privacy regulations and best practices.
  - **Data Security:** Implementing robust security measures to protect data from unauthorized access and breaches.

- **Transparency and Accountability:**
  - **Explainability:** Ensuring that machine learning models are interpretable and their decisions can be explained to stakeholders.
  - **Accountability:** Establishing clear accountability for data science practices and ensuring that ethical standards are maintained.

Data Science Project Lifecycle

The data science project lifecycle encompasses the entire process of developing and deploying data science solutions, from problem formulation to model deployment and monitoring.

1. **Problem Formulation:**
   - Defining the business problem and objectives.
   - Identifying the data science techniques required to address the problem.
2. **Data Collection and Preprocessing:**
   - Gathering relevant data from various sources.
   - Cleaning, transforming, and preparing the data for analysis.
3. **Exploratory Data Analysis (EDA):**

- Analyzing the data to understand its characteristics and uncover patterns.
- Visualizing the data to gain insights and inform model selection.

4. **Model Development:**
   - Selecting appropriate machine learning algorithms.
   - Training and validating the models using cross-validation techniques.

5. **Model Evaluation and Optimization:**
   - Evaluating model performance using relevant metrics.
   - Tuning hyperparameters to optimize model performance.

6. **Model Deployment:**
   - Deploying the model in a production environment.
   - Integrating the model with existing systems and workflows.

7. **Model Monitoring and Maintenance:**
   - Monitoring the model's performance over time.
   - Updating and retraining the model as needed to maintain accuracy and relevance.

CONCLUSION

Chapter 13 explores the practical applications of data science through real-world case studies, industry-specific use cases, ethical considerations, and the data science project lifecycle. By understanding these aspects, you will be better equipped to apply data science techniques to address complex problems, drive business value, and ensure responsible and ethical use of data.

CHAPTER 14: DATA VISUALIZATION AND STORYTELLING

Principles of Effective Data Visualization

Data visualization is the graphical representation of data, which helps to uncover patterns, trends, and insights that might not be immediately obvious in raw data. Effective data visualization is crucial for communicating complex information clearly and efficiently.

- **Clarity:** The visualization should convey the message clearly, avoiding unnecessary complexity. Simplicity helps in understanding the data quickly.
- **Accuracy:** The visual representation should accurately reflect the data without distorting the information. Misleading scales, improper use of graphs, and omitted data points can lead to incorrect interpretations.
- **Relevance:** Visualizations should be relevant to the audience and the context. Tailor the visual representation to the needs and interests of the audience.
- **Consistency:** Use consistent color schemes, fonts, and labeling to maintain coherence across visualizations.
- **Aesthetics:** An aesthetically pleasing visualization can capture the audience's attention and make the data more

engaging. However, aesthetics should not compromise clarity or accuracy.

Tools for Creating Visualizations

Various tools are available for creating data visualizations, each with its unique features and capabilities. Some popular tools include:

- **Matplotlib and Seaborn (Python):**
    - **Matplotlib:** A versatile library for creating static, interactive, and animated visualizations in Python. It provides extensive customization options.
    - **Seaborn:** Built on top of Matplotlib, Seaborn offers a high-level interface for creating attractive and informative statistical graphics with minimal code.
- **ggplot2 (R):**
    - **Overview:** A powerful data visualization package in R based on the Grammar of Graphics, allowing users to create complex and multi-layered visualizations.
    - **Features:** Simplifies the creation of plots by breaking down graphs into semantic components such as scales, layers, and themes.
- **Tableau:**
    - **Overview:** A leading data visualization tool that enables users to create interactive and shareable dashboards. It connects to various data sources and provides drag-and-drop functionality for building visualizations.
    - **Features:** Offers extensive customization options, supports real-time data integration, and provides a wide range of visualization types.
- **Power BI:**

- **Overview:** A business analytics tool by Microsoft that allows users to create interactive visualizations and business intelligence reports.
- **Features:** Integrates with various data sources, offers drag-and-drop functionality, and supports real-time data updates and sharing.

- **D3.js:**
  - **Overview:** A JavaScript library for creating dynamic, interactive data visualizations in web browsers. D3.js leverages HTML, SVG, and CSS to bring data to life.
  - **Features:** Provides fine-grained control over the visual elements, enabling the creation of highly customized and interactive visualizations.

Crafting Data-Driven Stories

Data storytelling is the practice of building a narrative around data and its analysis to communicate insights effectively. It combines data visualization with contextual information to tell a compelling story.

- **Identify the Key Message:**
  - Determine the central insight or finding that you want to convey through your data. Focus on a clear and concise message that resonates with your audience.
- **Use a Structured Narrative:**
  - Craft a narrative structure that guides the audience through the data, providing context and explanations along the way. A typical structure includes an introduction, the main findings, supporting evidence, and a conclusion.
- **Incorporate Visualizations:**
  - Use visualizations to support your narrative, making complex data more understandable and

engaging. Ensure that each visualization aligns with the key message and contributes to the overall story.

- **Provide Context:**
  - Contextualize the data by explaining its relevance and significance. Include background information, comparisons, and real-world implications to help the audience understand the impact of the data.
- **Engage the Audience:**
  - Use storytelling techniques to capture and maintain the audience's attention. Incorporate anecdotes, quotes, and examples to make the data more relatable and memorable.

Communicating Insights to Stakeholders

Effectively communicating data insights to stakeholders is crucial for driving informed decision-making. Here are some best practices for presenting data to different audiences:

- **Know Your Audience:**
  - Understand the needs, interests, and expertise of your audience. Tailor your presentation to their level of understanding and focus on the insights that are most relevant to them.
- **Simplify Complex Information:**
  - Break down complex data into easily digestible pieces. Use clear and straightforward language, avoiding technical jargon that might confuse the audience.
- **Focus on Key Takeaways:**
  - Highlight the most important insights and recommendations. Emphasize the actionable findings that stakeholders can use to make decisions.

- **Use Visual Aids:**
    - Incorporate visual aids such as charts, graphs, and infographics to enhance understanding and retention. Ensure that the visualizations are clear, accurate, and aligned with the key message.
- **Practice Effective Presentation Skills:**
    - Deliver your presentation with confidence and clarity. Use a logical flow, maintain eye contact, and engage with your audience through questions and discussions.
- **Follow-Up with Documentation:**
    - Provide stakeholders with detailed documentation of the analysis and findings. This allows them to review the information at their own pace and refer back to it as needed.

CONCLUSION

Chapter 14 explores the principles of effective data visualization, tools for creating visualizations, crafting data-driven stories, and communicating insights to stakeholders. By mastering these techniques, you will be able to convey complex information clearly and compellingly, enabling your audience to understand and act on data-driven insights.

CHAPTER 15: INTRODUCTION TO ARTIFICIAL INTELLIGENCE

Overview of Artificial Intelligence (AI)

Artificial Intelligence (AI) is a branch of computer science that aims to create machines capable of performing tasks that typically require human intelligence. These tasks include reasoning, learning, problem-solving, perception, language understanding, and more. AI has become an integral part of many industries, transforming how we interact with technology and enabling new capabilities.

- **Types of AI:**
    - **Narrow AI:** Also known as Weak AI, this type is designed and trained for a specific task. Examples include virtual assistants like Siri and Alexa, and recommendation systems like those used by Netflix and Amazon.
    - **General AI:** Also known as Strong AI, this type has the ability to understand, learn, and apply knowledge across a wide range of tasks, similar to human intelligence. General AI remains a theoretical concept and has not yet been

achieved.

Relationship Between AI and Data Science

AI and data science are closely related fields that often overlap. Data science involves extracting insights and knowledge from data using various techniques, including statistics, machine learning, and data visualization. AI, particularly machine learning, is a key component of data science that enables machines to learn from data and make predictions or decisions.

- **Data Science vs. AI:**
    - **Data Science:** Focuses on analyzing data to extract insights, identify patterns, and inform decision-making. It involves data collection, preprocessing, analysis, visualization, and interpretation.
    - **AI:** Focuses on creating intelligent systems that can perform tasks autonomously. It includes machine learning, natural language processing, computer vision, robotics, and other subfields.
- **Intersection:** Machine learning, a subfield of AI, is a crucial part of data science. It enables data scientists to build predictive models and algorithms that can learn from data and improve over time.

Key AI Technologies and Trends

AI encompasses a wide range of technologies and techniques that are constantly evolving. Key AI technologies and trends include:

- **Machine Learning (ML):** A subset of AI that involves training algorithms to learn from data and make predictions or decisions. ML techniques include supervised learning, unsupervised learning, reinforcement learning, and deep learning.
- **Natural Language Processing (NLP):** Enables machines to understand, interpret, and generate human language. NLP applications include language translation, sentiment analysis, chatbots, and text summarization.

- **Computer Vision:** Enables machines to interpret and analyze visual information from the world, such as images and videos. Applications include facial recognition, object detection, image segmentation, and autonomous vehicles.
- **Robotics:** Involves the design and development of robots that can perform tasks autonomously or semi-autonomously. Robotics applications include manufacturing automation, healthcare robots, and drones.
- **Deep Learning:** A subset of machine learning that involves training deep neural networks with many layers to capture complex patterns and representations. Deep learning has achieved state-of-the-art performance in various AI tasks, such as image recognition and natural language processing.
- **Generative Adversarial Networks (GANs):** A type of deep learning model that involves two neural networks, a generator and a discriminator, competing against each other. GANs are used for generating realistic synthetic data, such as images, text, and audio.
- **Reinforcement Learning:** A type of machine learning where agents learn to make decisions by interacting with an environment and receiving feedback in the form of rewards or penalties. Applications include game playing, robotics, and autonomous systems.

Future of AI in Data Science

The future of AI in data science is promising, with advancements in technology and increasing access to data driving innovation and new applications. Key trends and future directions include:

- **AI-Driven Automation:** AI will continue to automate various data science tasks, such as data cleaning, feature engineering, and model selection, increasing efficiency and reducing the need for manual intervention.

- **Explainable AI (XAI):** As AI models become more complex, the need for transparency and interpretability grows. XAI aims to create models that provide clear explanations for their decisions, improving trust and accountability.
- **AI Ethics and Fairness:** Ensuring that AI systems are fair, unbiased, and ethical is crucial. Future developments will focus on creating frameworks and guidelines to address ethical considerations and mitigate biases in AI.
- **AI in Edge Computing:** AI algorithms will increasingly be deployed on edge devices, such as smartphones and IoT devices, enabling real-time processing and decision-making without relying on cloud infrastructure.
- **AI-Enhanced Human Collaboration:** AI will augment human capabilities, enabling more effective collaboration between humans and machines. AI-driven tools will assist data scientists in making better decisions and uncovering insights.

CONCLUSION

Chapter 15 provides an introduction to artificial intelligence, exploring its relationship with data science, key technologies and trends, and the future of AI in data science. By understanding these concepts, you will gain a deeper appreciation of AI's role in transforming data science and driving innovation across various industries.

CHAPTER 16: DEEP LEARNING AND NEURAL NETWORKS

Fundamentals of Neural Networks

Neural networks are a class of machine learning models inspired by the structure and function of the human brain. They consist of interconnected layers of neurons that process and learn from data. The fundamental components of neural networks include:

- **Neurons:** Basic units that perform computations, passing signals through activation functions.
- **Layers:** Organized groups of neurons, including input, hidden, and output layers.
- **Weights and Biases:** Parameters that are adjusted during training to minimize the error between predicted and actual values.
- **Activation Functions:** Non-linear functions applied to neuron outputs, enabling neural networks to capture complex patterns (e.g., ReLU, Sigmoid, Tanh).

Convolutional Neural Networks (CNNs)

Convolutional Neural Networks (CNNs) are specialized neural networks designed for processing grid-like data, such as images. They use convolutional layers to automatically and adaptively learn spatial hierarchies of features from input images.

- **Key Components:**

- **Convolutional Layers:** Apply convolutional filters to the input data, detecting local patterns such as edges, textures, and shapes.
- **Pooling Layers:** Reduce the dimensionality of the data by down-sampling, preserving important features while reducing computation.
- **Fully Connected Layers:** Connect all neurons from the previous layer to the current layer, used for high-level reasoning and decision-making.
- **Dropout:** A regularization technique that randomly drops neurons during training to prevent overfitting.
- **Applications:** CNNs are widely used in image recognition, object detection, image segmentation, and video analysis.

Recurrent Neural Networks (RNNs)

Recurrent Neural Networks (RNNs) are designed for sequential data, such as time series or text, with connections forming directed cycles to capture temporal dependencies. RNNs can use their internal state (memory) to process sequences of inputs.

- **Key Components:**
    - **Recurrent Connections:** Connections between neurons in the same layer that enable the network to maintain a memory of previous inputs.
    - **Hidden States:** Represent the memory of the network, capturing information about previous time steps.
    - **LSTM (Long Short-Term Memory):** A type of RNN that addresses the vanishing gradient problem, allowing the network to capture long-

term dependencies. It uses gating mechanisms (input gate, forget gate, and output gate) to control the flow of information.
- **GRU (Gated Recurrent Unit):** A simplified version of LSTM that also captures long-term dependencies but with fewer parameters.
- **Applications:** RNNs are used in natural language processing, speech recognition, time series forecasting, and sequence generation.

Advanced Deep Learning Architectures

Deep learning has evolved to include various advanced architectures that push the boundaries of what neural networks can achieve. Some notable architectures include:

- **Transformers:**
  - **Overview:** A deep learning model architecture that relies on self-attention mechanisms to process input sequences in parallel, rather than sequentially.
  - **Key Components:**
    - **Self-Attention:** Computes the relevance of each word in a sequence to every other word, capturing long-range dependencies.
    - **Multi-Head Attention:** Enhances the model's ability to focus on different parts of the input sequence simultaneously.
    - **Positional Encoding:** Adds information about the position of each word in the sequence, as transformers do not inherently capture order.
  - **Applications:** Transformers are widely used in natural language processing tasks, such as

machine translation, text summarization, and question answering. Notable models include BERT, GPT, and T5.

- **Generative Adversarial Networks (GANs):**
    - **Overview:** GANs consist of two neural networks, a generator and a discriminator, that compete against each other in a zero-sum game. The generator creates synthetic data, while the discriminator evaluates its authenticity.
    - **Key Components:**
        - **Generator:** Produces synthetic data from random noise, aiming to create realistic samples.
        - **Discriminator:** Distinguishes between real and synthetic data, providing feedback to the generator.
    - **Applications:** GANs are used for image generation, data augmentation, style transfer, and generating realistic synthetic data (e.g., deepfakes).
- **Autoencoders:**
    - **Overview:** Autoencoders are neural networks designed to learn efficient representations of input data by compressing it into a lower-dimensional latent space and then reconstructing it.
    - **Key Components:**
        - **Encoder:** Maps the input data to a lower-dimensional latent space.
        - **Decoder:** Reconstructs the input data from the latent representation.
    - **Variational Autoencoders (VAEs):** A type of autoencoder that introduces probabilistic

modeling, enabling the generation of new data samples.

- **Applications:** Autoencoders are used for dimensionality reduction, anomaly detection, data denoising, and generative modeling.

CONCLUSION

Chapter 16 delves into the fundamentals of deep learning and neural networks, exploring key architectures such as Convolutional Neural Networks (CNNs), Recurrent Neural Networks (RNNs), and advanced models like Transformers, Generative Adversarial Networks (GANs), and Autoencoders. By understanding these deep learning techniques, you will be equipped to tackle complex data science problems and leverage cutting-edge technologies to extract valuable insights and create innovative solutions.

CHAPTER 17: NATURAL LANGUAGE PROCESSING (NLP)

Text Data Preprocessing

Natural Language Processing (NLP) involves the interaction between computers and human language, enabling machines to understand, interpret, and generate text. Preprocessing text data is a crucial step in NLP to prepare the data for analysis and model building.

- **Tokenization:** Splitting text into individual words or tokens. This can be done at different levels:
    - **Word Tokenization:** Splitting text into individual words.
    - **Sentence Tokenization:** Splitting text into individual sentences.
- **Normalization:** Converting text to a standard format, which includes:
    - **Lowercasing:** Converting all text to lowercase to ensure uniformity.
    - **Removing Punctuation:** Eliminating punctuation marks to avoid treating them as separate tokens.
    - **Removing Special Characters:** Cleaning text by removing symbols and special characters.

- **Stop Words Removal:** Removing common words that do not carry significant meaning (e.g., "the", "and", "is") to focus on more meaningful words.
- **Stemming and Lemmatization:**
    - **Stemming:** Reducing words to their base or root forms by removing suffixes (e.g., "running" to "run").
    - **Lemmatization:** Converting words to their base or dictionary form (lemma) based on context (e.g., "better" to "good").
- **Text Vectorization:** Converting text into numerical representations for machine learning models.
    - **Bag-of-Words (BoW):** Represents text as a vector of word counts.
    - **Term Frequency-Inverse Document Frequency (TF-IDF):** Represents text based on word importance relative to the entire corpus.
    - **Word Embeddings:** Dense vector representations of words that capture semantic meaning (e.g., Word2Vec, GloVe).

Sentiment Analysis

Sentiment analysis is a common NLP task that involves determining the sentiment or emotion expressed in text. It helps in understanding opinions, attitudes, and feelings from textual data.

- **Approaches:**
    - **Rule-Based:** Uses predefined rules and lexicons to classify text based on sentiment-bearing words.
    - **Machine Learning:** Trains models on labeled datasets to predict sentiment.
    - **Deep Learning:** Utilizes neural networks, such as LSTM or transformers, to capture complex

patterns in text for sentiment prediction.
- **Applications:**
    - **Customer Feedback:** Analyzing reviews, surveys, and social media posts to gauge customer sentiment.
    - **Market Analysis:** Understanding public sentiment towards products, brands, or events.
    - **Social Media Monitoring:** Tracking sentiment trends on platforms like Twitter and Facebook.

Text Classification and Clustering

Text classification and clustering are essential NLP tasks that involve categorizing and grouping text data based on their content.

- **Text Classification:**
    - **Supervised Learning:** Training models on labeled data to classify text into predefined categories (e.g., spam detection, topic categorization).
    - **Algorithms:** Naive Bayes, Support Vector Machines (SVM), Decision Trees, and deep learning models like CNNs and RNNs.
    - **Applications:** Email filtering, news categorization, document classification.
- **Text Clustering:**
    - **Unsupervised Learning:** Grouping similar documents or text snippets without predefined labels.
    - **Algorithms:** K-Means, Hierarchical Clustering, DBSCAN.
    - **Applications:** Document clustering, topic modeling, customer segmentation.

Advanced NLP Techniques

Advanced NLP techniques leverage deep learning models and sophisticated algorithms to achieve state-of-the-art performance in various NLP tasks.

- **Transformers:**
    - **Overview:** A deep learning architecture that relies on self-attention mechanisms to process input sequences in parallel.
    - **Key Models:** BERT (Bidirectional Encoder Representations from Transformers), GPT (Generative Pre-trained Transformer), T5 (Text-to-Text Transfer Transformer).
    - **Applications:** Machine translation, text summarization, question answering, language generation.
- **Named Entity Recognition (NER):**
    - **Overview:** Identifying and classifying named entities (e.g., people, organizations, locations) in text.
    - **Approaches:** Rule-based, machine learning, and deep learning methods.
    - **Applications:** Information extraction, content categorization, knowledge graph construction.
- **Text Generation:**
    - **Overview:** Generating coherent and contextually relevant text based on input data.
    - **Techniques:** Recurrent Neural Networks (RNNs), LSTM, Transformers.
    - **Applications:** Chatbots, creative writing, automated content generation.

CONCLUSION

Chapter 17 explores the key concepts and techniques of Natural Language Processing (NLP), including text data preprocessing, sentiment analysis, text classification and clustering, and advanced NLP methods. By mastering these techniques, you will be equipped to work with textual data, extract valuable insights, and build sophisticated NLP models for various applications.

CHAPTER 18: REINFORCEMENT LEARNING

Basics of Reinforcement Learning

Reinforcement Learning (RL) is a type of machine learning where an agent learns to make decisions by interacting with an environment and receiving feedback in the form of rewards or penalties. The goal is to develop a policy that maximizes the cumulative reward over time.

- **Key Concepts:**
    - **Agent:** The learner or decision-maker that interacts with the environment.
    - **Environment:** The system or world with which the agent interacts.
    - **State:** A representation of the current situation of the environment.
    - **Action:** A decision or move made by the agent that affects the state.
    - **Reward:** Feedback received from the environment in response to an action, indicating the immediate benefit.
    - **Policy:** A strategy that the agent follows to decide actions based on the current state.
    - **Value Function:** A function that estimates the

expected cumulative reward of being in a state or taking an action in a state.

Key Concepts and Algorithms

Reinforcement learning involves several key concepts and algorithms that enable agents to learn optimal policies through trial and error.

- **Markov Decision Process (MDP):**
    - **Overview:** A mathematical framework for modeling decision-making problems. It includes a set of states (S), a set of actions (A), a reward function (R), and a state transition probability function (P).
    - **Objective:** Maximize the cumulative reward (return) over time, often expressed as the expected sum of discounted rewards.
- **Q-Learning:**
    - **Overview:** A value-based RL algorithm that aims to learn the optimal action-value function (Q-function) without requiring a model of the environment.
    - **Key Equation:** The Q-function is updated using the Bellman equation:

$$Q(s,a) \leftarrow Q(s,a) + \alpha \left(r + \gamma \max_{a'} Q(s', a') - Q(s, a) \right)$$

where α is the learning rate, γ is the discount factor, r is the reward, and s' is the next state.

- **Exploration vs. Exploitation:** Balancing the exploration of new actions with the exploitation of known actions to maximize the reward.
- **Deep Q-Learning (DQN):**
    - **Overview:** An extension of Q-learning that uses deep neural networks to approximate the Q-function, enabling the handling of large state

and action spaces.
- **Key Components:**
  - **Experience Replay:** Storing past experiences in a replay buffer and sampling from it to break the correlation between consecutive updates.
  - **Target Network:** A separate network to stabilize the training by reducing the oscillations in Q-value estimates.
- **Policy Gradient Methods:**
  - **Overview:** Directly optimize the policy by adjusting the parameters to maximize the expected reward.
  - **REINFORCE Algorithm:** A basic policy gradient method that updates the policy parameters in the direction of the gradient of the expected reward.
  - **Actor-Critic Methods:** Combine policy gradient methods (actor) with value function approximation (critic) to reduce variance and improve training stability.

Applications of Reinforcement Learning

Reinforcement learning has a wide range of applications across various domains, demonstrating its versatility and effectiveness in solving complex decision-making problems.
- **Game Playing:**
  - **Chess and Go:** RL agents, such as AlphaGo, have achieved superhuman performance in board games by learning optimal strategies through self-play.
  - **Video Games:** RL agents can learn to play video games, often surpassing human performance, as demonstrated by agents developed by

DeepMind and OpenAI.
- **Robotics:**
    - **Robot Control:** RL is used to train robots for tasks like manipulation, locomotion, and navigation, enabling them to adapt to dynamic environments.
    - **Autonomous Vehicles:** RL agents learn to make driving decisions, improving the performance and safety of autonomous vehicles.
- **Natural Language Processing (NLP):**
    - **Dialogue Systems:** RL is used to optimize dialogue policies in conversational agents and chatbots, enhancing their ability to interact with users.
    - **Machine Translation:** RL improves translation quality by fine-tuning models based on feedback from human evaluators.
- **Finance:**
    - **Portfolio Management:** RL agents learn to make investment decisions that maximize returns while managing risk.
    - **Algorithmic Trading:** RL is applied to develop trading strategies that adapt to market conditions and optimize trading performance.

Challenges and Future Directions

While reinforcement learning has shown great promise, it also faces several challenges that require ongoing research and development.

- **Sample Efficiency:** RL algorithms often require large amounts of data and interactions with the environment to learn effective policies. Improving sample efficiency is a key area of research.
- **Exploration Strategies:** Balancing exploration and

exploitation remains a challenge, especially in environments with large or continuous action spaces.
- **Generalization:** Ensuring that RL agents generalize well to new, unseen states and environments is crucial for their robustness and applicability.
- **Safety and Ethics:** Ensuring the safe and ethical deployment of RL agents, particularly in high-stakes or real-world applications, is an important consideration.

Future directions in reinforcement learning research include developing more sample-efficient algorithms, improving exploration strategies, enhancing generalization capabilities, and addressing safety and ethical concerns.

CONCLUSION

Chapter 18 provides an in-depth exploration of reinforcement learning, covering the basics, key concepts and algorithms, practical applications, and challenges. By understanding these aspects, you will be equipped to develop RL agents that can solve complex decision-making problems and drive innovation across various domains.

CHAPTER 19: ETHICS AND BIAS IN DATA SCIENCE

Understanding Bias and Fairness

Bias in data science refers to systematic errors that can lead to unfair outcomes and inaccuracies in data analysis and model predictions. These biases can stem from various sources, such as data collection, data preprocessing, model selection, and human judgment. Fairness in data science aims to mitigate these biases and ensure equitable treatment for all individuals and groups.

- **Types of Bias:**
    - **Selection Bias:** Arises when the sample data is not representative of the population, leading to skewed results.
    - **Measurement Bias:** Occurs when data is inaccurately measured or recorded, affecting the quality and reliability of the data.
    - **Confirmation Bias:** Happens when researchers or analysts unintentionally favor data that supports their preconceived notions or hypotheses.
    - **Algorithmic Bias:** Results from the algorithms themselves, which may inadvertently favor certain groups over others due to their design or

training data.
- **Fairness Metrics:**
    - **Demographic Parity:** Ensuring that model predictions are independent of protected attributes, such as race or gender.
    - **Equal Opportunity:** Ensuring that individuals from different groups have equal chances of receiving positive outcomes if they qualify.
    - **Calibration:** Ensuring that predicted probabilities accurately reflect the true likelihood of outcomes across different groups.

Ethical Implications of Data Science

Ethical considerations in data science involve ensuring that data practices respect privacy, uphold transparency, and do not cause harm. Addressing ethical concerns is crucial for maintaining public trust and ensuring responsible use of data.

- **Privacy and Confidentiality:**
    - **Data Anonymization:** Removing personally identifiable information (PII) from datasets to protect individuals' privacy.
    - **Informed Consent:** Ensuring that individuals are aware of how their data will be used and have given explicit permission.
    - **Data Security:** Implementing robust security measures to protect data from unauthorized access and breaches.
- **Transparency and Accountability:**
    - **Explainability:** Making model decisions transparent and understandable to stakeholders, ensuring that the reasoning behind predictions is clear.
    - **Accountability:** Establishing clear lines of responsibility for data practices and ensuring

that ethical standards are upheld throughout the data lifecycle.
- **Avoiding Harm:**
    - **Non-Discrimination:** Ensuring that data science practices do not lead to discriminatory outcomes or reinforce existing biases.
    - **Impact Assessment:** Evaluating the potential impact of data science projects on individuals and society, and taking steps to mitigate negative effects.

Best Practices for Ethical Data Science

To address bias and ethical concerns, data scientists should adopt best practices that promote fairness, transparency, and accountability.

- **Diverse and Representative Data:**
    - **Data Collection:** Ensure that the data collected is diverse and representative of the population to avoid selection bias.
    - **Data Augmentation:** Use techniques such as data augmentation and synthetic data generation to address imbalances in the dataset.
- **Bias Detection and Mitigation:**
    - **Bias Audits:** Regularly audit datasets and models for potential biases and take corrective actions as needed.
    - **Fairness Constraints:** Incorporate fairness constraints into model training to ensure equitable outcomes.
    - **Adversarial Debiasing:** Use adversarial techniques to train models that are less sensitive to bias.
- **Transparent and Explainable Models:**
    - **Model Interpretability:** Use interpretable

models or techniques like LIME and SHAP to explain model predictions.
    - **Documentation:** Maintain thorough documentation of data sources, preprocessing steps, model decisions, and evaluation metrics.
- **Ethical Decision-Making:**
    - **Ethics Committees:** Establish ethics committees to review data science projects and ensure compliance with ethical standards.
    - **Guidelines and Frameworks:** Follow established ethical guidelines and frameworks, such as the EU's General Data Protection Regulation (GDPR) and the IEEE's Ethically Aligned Design.

Addressing Bias in Machine Learning Models

Addressing bias in machine learning models involves identifying, quantifying, and mitigating biases to ensure fair and accurate predictions.

- **Identifying Bias:**
    - **Exploratory Data Analysis (EDA):** Use EDA techniques to identify potential sources of bias in the data.
    - **Fairness Metrics:** Calculate fairness metrics to assess the presence and extent of bias in model predictions.
- **Quantifying Bias:**
    - **Statistical Tests:** Use statistical tests, such as chi-square tests, to quantify bias in the data and model outcomes.
    - **Disparity Ratios:** Measure the disparity in outcomes between different groups to quantify bias.
- **Mitigating Bias:**
    - **Preprocessing:** Address bias during data

preprocessing by reweighting, resampling, or transforming the data to reduce bias.
- **In-Processing:** Incorporate fairness constraints into the model training process to enforce equitable treatment.
- **Post-Processing:** Adjust model predictions after training to correct for any biases that remain.

CONCLUSION

Chapter 19 delves into the critical aspects of ethics and bias in data science, highlighting the importance of understanding and addressing biases, ethical implications, and best practices for ethical data science. By adopting these principles and techniques, you will be equipped to conduct data science responsibly and fairly, ensuring that your work has a positive impact on individuals and society.

CHAPTER 20: CAPSTONE PROJECT

Project Planning and Execution

The capstone project is a culmination of your journey through this data science course. It provides an opportunity to apply the knowledge and skills you have acquired to a real-world problem, demonstrating your proficiency in data science. The project involves several stages, from planning to execution, and requires a thorough understanding of the data science workflow.

- **Define the Problem:**
    - **Identify a Relevant Problem:** Choose a problem that is significant and relevant to your area of interest or industry.
    - **Set Clear Objectives:** Define what you aim to achieve with your project, including specific questions you want to answer or hypotheses you want to test.
- **Data Collection and Preprocessing:**
    - **Gather Data:** Collect data from relevant sources, ensuring it is sufficient and relevant for your analysis.
    - **Clean and Prepare Data:** Preprocess the data to handle missing values, outliers, and inconsistencies. This step also includes data transformation and feature engineering.

- **Exploratory Data Analysis (EDA):**
    - **Analyze Data:** Conduct EDA to understand the data's characteristics, distributions, and relationships between variables.
    - **Visualize Data:** Use data visualization techniques to uncover patterns and insights that will guide your modeling decisions.
- **Model Development:**
    - **Select Algorithms:** Choose appropriate machine learning or statistical algorithms based on the problem and data characteristics.
    - **Train Models:** Train multiple models using the prepared data, adjusting parameters to optimize performance.
    - **Evaluate Models:** Assess model performance using relevant metrics and cross-validation techniques. Compare models to select the best-performing one.
- **Model Deployment:**
    - **Implement the Model:** Deploy the chosen model in a production environment, ensuring it is accessible and usable for stakeholders.
    - **Integrate with Systems:** Integrate the model with existing systems or workflows to ensure seamless operation and utility.

Data Collection and Preprocessing

The success of your capstone project hinges on the quality of the data you collect and how well you preprocess it. This stage involves several critical steps:

- **Data Sources:**
    - **Internal Databases:** Leverage existing data within your organization, such as CRM systems, transaction records, and operational databases.

- **Public Datasets:** Utilize publicly available datasets from government websites, research institutions, and open data platforms.
- **Web Scraping:** Extract data from websites using web scraping tools and techniques, ensuring compliance with legal and ethical guidelines.
- **APIs:** Access data through APIs provided by various services and platforms, such as social media, financial data providers, and weather services.

- **Data Cleaning:**
  - **Handle Missing Values:** Address missing data by imputing values, removing incomplete records, or using advanced techniques like KNN imputation.
  - **Remove Outliers:** Identify and remove outliers that can skew analysis and model performance.
  - **Standardize Data:** Normalize or standardize data to ensure consistent scales across features.
- **Data Transformation:**
  - **Feature Engineering:** Create new features that capture important information and enhance model performance. This may include aggregating data, creating interaction terms, or transforming variables.
  - **Encoding Categorical Variables:** Convert categorical data into numerical format using techniques like one-hot encoding, label encoding, or binary encoding.

Model Development and Evaluation

Developing and evaluating models is at the heart of your capstone project. This stage involves selecting, training, and fine-tuning models to achieve the best performance.

- **Model Selection:**
    - **Algorithm Choice:** Select algorithms that are well-suited to the problem, considering factors such as the type of data, problem complexity, and interpretability requirements.
    - **Baseline Models:** Start with simple baseline models to set a performance benchmark.
- **Model Training:**
    - **Train-Test Split:** Divide the data into training and test sets to evaluate model performance on unseen data.
    - **Cross-Validation:** Use cross-validation techniques to ensure robustness and avoid overfitting.
    - **Hyperparameter Tuning:** Optimize model parameters using grid search, random search, or Bayesian optimization to improve performance.
- **Model Evaluation:**
    - **Performance Metrics:** Use appropriate metrics to evaluate model performance, such as accuracy, precision, recall, F1-score, RMSE, or AUC.
    - **Comparison:** Compare different models to select the one that best meets the project's objectives.
    - **Model Interpretation:** Ensure the model is interpretable and its predictions can be explained to stakeholders.

Presentation and Documentation

Effectively presenting and documenting your capstone project is crucial for demonstrating your findings and ensuring that your work can be reviewed and replicated.

- **Presentation:**
    - **Visual Storytelling:** Use visualizations to tell a

compelling story, highlighting key insights and results.
- **Clear Communication:** Present your findings in a clear and concise manner, ensuring that your audience understands the significance of your work.
- **Stakeholder Engagement:** Tailor your presentation to the needs and interests of your audience, whether they are technical experts or business stakeholders.

- **Documentation:**
  - **Project Report:** Prepare a comprehensive report detailing the problem, methodology, data, analysis, models, results, and conclusions.
  - **Code and Notebooks:** Provide well-documented code and Jupyter notebooks to allow others to reproduce your analysis and results.
  - **Appendices:** Include supplementary materials, such as raw data, additional analyses, and references to relevant literature.

CONCLUSION

Chapter 20 guides you through the process of completing a capstone project, from planning and data collection to model development, evaluation, and presentation. By following these steps, you will demonstrate your proficiency in data science and showcase your ability to solve real-world problems using data-driven approaches.

CHAPTER 21: FUTURE TRENDS IN DATA SCIENCE

Emerging Technologies and Techniques

The field of data science is constantly evolving, with new technologies and techniques emerging to address complex challenges and unlock new opportunities. Staying informed about these trends is crucial for data scientists to remain competitive and innovative.

- **Artificial Intelligence (AI) and Machine Learning (ML) Advances:**
    - **AutoML:** Automated Machine Learning (AutoML) simplifies the process of building and deploying machine learning models by automating tasks such as feature engineering, model selection, and hyperparameter tuning.
    - **Federated Learning:** A collaborative approach to machine learning where models are trained across multiple decentralized devices or servers while preserving data privacy.
    - **Explainable AI (XAI):** Techniques and tools that make AI models more transparent and interpretable, helping stakeholders understand and trust AI-driven decisions.

- **Big Data Technologies:**
  - **Edge Computing:** Processing data closer to the source (e.g., IoT devices) to reduce latency and bandwidth usage, enabling real-time analytics and decision-making.
  - **Quantum Computing:** Leveraging the principles of quantum mechanics to perform complex computations much faster than classical computers, with potential applications in optimization, cryptography, and large-scale data analysis.
- **Natural Language Processing (NLP) Innovations:**
  - **Transformers and BERT:** Continued advancements in transformer architectures and models like BERT (Bidirectional Encoder Representations from Transformers) for improved language understanding and generation.
  - **Conversational AI:** Enhanced capabilities in dialogue systems and chatbots for more natural and engaging human-computer interactions.

The Role of Data Science in Industry 4.0

Industry 4.0, also known as the Fourth Industrial Revolution, is characterized by the integration of advanced technologies such as AI, IoT, and robotics into manufacturing and industrial processes. Data science plays a pivotal role in this transformation by enabling:

- **Predictive Maintenance:** Using sensor data and machine learning algorithms to predict equipment failures and schedule maintenance proactively, reducing downtime and costs.
- **Smart Manufacturing:** Optimizing production processes through data-driven insights, improving efficiency, quality, and flexibility.

- **Supply Chain Optimization:** Enhancing supply chain visibility and decision-making through real-time data analytics and predictive modeling.

Data Privacy and Security

As data becomes increasingly valuable and ubiquitous, ensuring data privacy and security is paramount. Emerging trends and best practices in this area include:

- **Privacy-Preserving Techniques:**
    - **Differential Privacy:** Techniques that add noise to data or query results to protect individual privacy while enabling useful analysis.
    - **Homomorphic Encryption:** A form of encryption that allows computations to be performed on encrypted data without decrypting it, preserving data confidentiality.
- **Regulatory Compliance:**
    - **GDPR (General Data Protection Regulation):** A comprehensive data protection regulation in the EU that sets standards for data privacy and security.
    - **CCPA (California Consumer Privacy Act):** A state-level regulation in the US that provides consumers with rights over their personal data.
- **Data Governance:**
    - **Data Stewardship:** Assigning responsibility for managing data quality, privacy, and security within organizations.
    - **Data Auditing:** Regularly reviewing data practices and systems to ensure compliance with regulations and best practices.

Preparing for the Future of Data Science

To stay ahead in the rapidly evolving field of data science, it is essential to continuously update your skills and knowledge. Here

are some strategies for preparing for the future:
- **Lifelong Learning:**
    - **Online Courses and Certifications:** Enroll in courses on platforms like Coursera, edX, and Udacity to learn new skills and earn certifications.
    - **Workshops and Conferences:** Attend industry events, workshops, and conferences to stay informed about the latest trends and network with peers.
- **Interdisciplinary Collaboration:**
    - **Cross-Functional Teams:** Work with professionals from diverse fields, such as engineering, business, and design, to gain new perspectives and insights.
    - **Research and Development:** Engage in collaborative research projects with academic institutions and industry partners to drive innovation.
- **Building a Strong Foundation:**
    - **Fundamental Skills:** Master the core skills of data science, including statistics, programming, data visualization, and machine learning.
    - **Advanced Techniques:** Stay updated with cutting-edge techniques, such as deep learning, reinforcement learning, and AI ethics.

CONCLUSION

Chapter 21 explores the future trends in data science, highlighting emerging technologies, the role of data science in Industry 4.0, data privacy and security, and strategies for preparing for the future. By staying informed and continuously updating your skills, you will be well-equipped to navigate the dynamic landscape of data science and contribute to its ongoing evolution.

Congratulations on reaching the end of this comprehensive guide to data science! Your journey to mastering data science has equipped you with valuable knowledge and skills to tackle complex challenges and drive innovation. Keep exploring, learning, and applying your expertise to make a meaningful impact in the world of data science.

AFTERWORD

As we reach the conclusion of "Mastering Data Science: From Fundamentals to Advanced Techniques," I want to take a moment to reflect on the journey we've embarked on together. This book has aimed to equip you with a comprehensive understanding of data science, covering its vast landscape from basic principles to cutting-edge technologies.

Throughout these chapters, we've explored the essential tools and techniques that form the backbone of data science. We've delved into machine learning, deep learning, and natural language processing, uncovering the power and potential of these advanced methodologies. We've examined practical applications across various industries, demonstrating how data science can transform real-world problems into opportunities for innovation and growth.

The capstone project provided a hands-on experience to apply your knowledge, bridging the gap between theory and practice. It served as a testament to your ability to tackle complex challenges, analyze data, and derive meaningful insights that can drive impactful decisions.

Moreover, we've underscored the importance of ethics and fairness in data science. As practitioners, it is our responsibility to ensure that the technologies we develop and the analyses we conduct are not only accurate but also equitable and just. Addressing biases and upholding ethical standards are critical for maintaining public trust and fostering a positive impact on society.

As the field of data science continues to evolve, staying curious and committed to lifelong learning will be your greatest assets. Embrace new technologies, explore emerging trends, and collaborate with interdisciplinary teams to broaden your horizons. The future of data science holds immense promise, and your contributions will shape its trajectory.

I hope this book has inspired and empowered you to continue your journey in data science with confidence and enthusiasm. Remember, the quest for knowledge is never-ending, and every challenge presents an opportunity to grow and innovate.

Thank you for embarking on this journey with me. I wish you all the best in your endeavors, and I look forward to seeing the incredible impact you will make in the world of data science.

Warm regards,

Yatendra Kumar Singh 'Manuh'

www.ingramcontent.com/pod-product-compliance
Lightning Source LLC
Chambersburg PA
CBHW071034240526
45469CB00006BD/2207